NEGATIVE EARTHLINGS EXPOSED

by

Marion H. Cureton

DORRANCE & COMPANY

Philadelphia

I wish to dedicate this book in memory of my beloved mother, Gladys Liethegner Stolle, who died July 22, 1959. The priceless heritage she has left me is my trusting, childlike faith and belief in God.

May I take this opportunity to express thanks and deep appreciation to all of the many good people who have been responsible for influencing my life for the better down through the years. The star of this show is my dear husband, Paul, who has given me the gift of self-confidence and belief in myself.

My three most precious treasures are son John, son Mark, and daughter Paula Marie. I am very grateful for the joys and complete fulfillment they have given me.

Without the help of all the wonderful members of my family and good friends, you would never be reading these words today.

Contents

Foreword vii

1 In the Beginning 1
2 Gravity of Negative Thought 5
3 Negative Satan versus Positive God 8
4 Negative Earthlings 12
5 A Positive Planet Perceived 17
6 Your Positive Response 26
7 Let Your Positive Light Shine 31
8 Meet the Big You Within 37
9 Take a Subconscious Trip 45
10 Earth's Return to the Positive 53

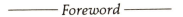 *Foreword* —

    With deep, sincere appreciation and thanks for the Holy Bible, which has given me such keen insight, and all students of positive thinking, especially the Most Reverend Archbishop Fulton J. Sheen, Dr. Norman Vincent Peale, Billy Graham, Unity School of Christianity, Dr. Alfred J. Cantor, Napoleon Hill and Harry Lorayne, who have shown me the importance of correct thought. It would be indeed impossible for you to be reading this book today without their help.

    Above all, I wish to give full credit to my faithful friend, my subconscious mind, who I believe is God within me. He provided all the creative ideas and inspiring words contained in this book. I simply told Him what kind of manuscript I wanted to write and He gave me the needed material. My name should not really be on the title page, because I was merely used as an instrument to bring positive thinking to a troubled world.

    I sincerely hope these simple, unsophisticated words will make you realize the importance of thought control, and may your good thoughts open up the doors of a whole new world of happiness for you.

    I am sure you will enjoy learning to know, love, and appreciate your subconscious mind as your dearest friend. Then you will confidently expect to find the power within yourself to solve all your problems. So, with great pleasure, I show you how to attain your goal.

Your friend,
Marion H. Cureton

1

In the Beginning

With great pleasure I bring hope to your troubled world. So whoever you are, wherever you may be, I want you to know that I am your good friend. I have come to bail you out of your present dire circumstances, which seem to be hopelessly imprisoning you this very moment. Even though you may already feel that you've reached the point of no return, I have to come to show you how to chart your course in the direction of success. You see, I am going to explain the use of a secret device locked deep inside your mind, which is guaranteed to change your destiny. It is indeed a pity to realize that only a very small minority of people are aware of their great power.

I hope you already feel the love, concern, and compassion I have for you. So I give you the warmth of my heart, bursting with love and understanding for your abode. Next, I offer you my open, outstretched arms, pleading with you to grasp them firmly, that together we can go down the road to victory. So let us start in the beginning.

The Divine Creator so loved men and women that He made them in His image and likeness. This means that He gave you an immortal soul, plus a mind exactly like His. Therefore, you, also, possess His powers of omnipotence and omniscience. However, there is only one ability Almighty God has beyond those of angels and human beings. It is His unique power to create something, from the very beginning, out of complete nothingness.

God was the very first person to show us how to correctly operate a creative mind. You see, He gave us six easy lessons during the time He made the universe. Proof of the above statement can be found in the first chapter of the Book of Genesis. Notice particularly the simple language God used to give positive direction to His creative mind, the subconscious. He also accompanied His words with very vivid mental images of whatever He desired His subconscious to create and with His confident spirit of expectancy. We, too, can use our subconscious minds in the same manner to obtain any good change for the better. We have the mind power to control whatever occurs in our lives. Thus, the future is pretty much in our own hands. There are only two factors in our lives which we are unable to control, and those are our birth and death. However, I believe many people die years before God intended to call them, because of their perpetual negative thinking.

Our human computer brain is indeed a magnificent masterpiece. God gave this great gift to the human race for a very definite purpose. He wanted people to solve their own problems from within. In the beginning, man was very much on his own and had to learn early in life how to stand on his feet to attain independence. You see, there were not many people around to help him. Therefore, it was very necessary for him to have a quick, easy method available on a moment's notice. I am sure this was God's reason for giving man a built-in device powered to fulfill all of his many special needs. Somehow, down through the ages of civilization, we have lost the art of using our great creative powers.

The modern-day computer is copied after your great computer brain, which consists of two minds, the conscious and the subconscious. Your conscious mind is the part of the brain where your personality lives and where the real you is found. We study, learn, memorize, analyze, pass judgment, and make decisions with it, too. The subconscious mind is your creative mind and contains a powerful force, which I believe is God within. It can be successfully used to change any bad situation to good.

Your computer brain works more efficiently when mind,

body, and spirit are united together in perfect harmony. The voice of your conscious mind feeds positive directions to your subconscious by means of simple commands. Then your conscious mind visualizes a clear picture in advance of the expected results and your spirit gives you the positive attitude of success. Finally, your loyal subconscious sends back the correct answer by giving you positive, creative ideas to make the necessary changes to insure favorable results.

It is my fondest hope that you will learn to love and appreciate your subconscious mind (God within you) as your most trusted and dearest friend. I can assure you that he is your faithful servant throughout your lifetime. He is always ready, willing, and able to respond immediately to your every beck and call and carries out all your orders to completion. He never sleeps a wink and automatically takes care of most of your bodily functions.

However, he is very much like a primitive animal mind and prefers simple commands best, accompanied with emotion. The spoken word is the fuel which is used to reach him. So guard your words, because he interprets every command literally and creates them as realities in your life. For example, never say repeatedly, "I'm feeling very sick"; rather, say, "I'm feeling much better and very soon will be well." Always give a positive suggestion along with a clear mental picture of what is desired and confidently expect quick results.

You will find that your subconscious mind works best while in a state of complete relaxation of mind, body, and spirit. So before giving him any kind of special command, it is best to say in advance, "Subconscious mind, you may relax now." Your goal will be obtained much sooner using this method. The very best time to talk to your good friend is just before going to sleep at night and upon awaking, having obtained a good rest.

I sincerely hope I have succeeded in showing you how to operate your great computer mind. The method is so simple that a very young child could easily learn to use it early in life. Would it not be wonderful if every child and adult throughout the world could receive this basic lesson in mind control.

So, in summing up the important points, we must approach the subconscious in a state of relaxation, use simple words to direct our commands, have very vivid mental pictures, and have complete confidence and belief in the expected outcome. The more frequently we feed to the mind positive affirmations accompanied with clear mental images and complete belief, the faster will be the action. Remember, repetition brings results.

2

Gravity of Negative Thought

Our Divine Creator was very wise indeed when He insisted that His Paradise of Heaven and His Garden of Paradise on Earth be forever places of positive thought. You see, He completely understood every intricate detail of the great computer brain, which He had created out of complete nothingness. Therefore, He knew in advance about the imbalance and damage this delicate instrument would suffer as the price of expressing just one negative thought. For this puts the conscious level of the mind under a great deal of pressure, entertaining both good and evil thoughts at the same time. Thus, it is forced into making the important decision regarding a correct choice. Remember, positive thoughts pull you up, while negative thoughts pull you down. Thus, having two entirely different kinds of thoughts in your conscious mind creates a state of confusion and a complete lack of harmony in your mind-body-spirit unit.

Your magnificent brain works very much like radio waves, because it transmits thoughts and receives them, too. You must remember that nothing has ever come into being without a thought behind it. However, God gave you free will, so it is entirely up to you to choose the type of thoughts you prefer to express. Your present living conditions and the state of your health today are the products of the predominant thinking of your many yesterdays.

You, and you alone, are the master of your own destiny. So guard your thoughts with great intensity, because your continuously repeated wrong choice will create adverse conditions in your life. Look upon negative thinking as a slow

5

poison that eventually kills your mind, body, and spirit in a vacuum of hopelessness.

Just as gravity forces heavy objects to fall, negative thinking brings your mental condition way down, too. Positive thinking raises your spirits and takes you up high in reach of Heaven's perfection, while negative thoughts force you down to the depths of despair. The only thing you can gain from perpetual negative thinking is more trouble. Worst of all, you not only hurt yourself, but cause everyone around you to be unhappy, too.

However, it is almost an impossibility to be completely positive in an environment of both positive and negative thought, because your brain has been wired both to send out thoughts and to receive them. Even if you decided now to habitually think only pure, good thoughts for the rest of your life, the negative thinking of others would be picked up by you and you would immediately feel their adverse interference.

Most Earthlings are predominantly negative thinkers. Looking upon the many deplorable conditions existing in today's world proves the truth of the above statement. However the minority of positive thinkers are indeed doing a great service to mankind by bringing their light of hope to the troubled world. Their good efforts are constantly being set back by the major downward pull of the gravity of negative thinking.

You must determine now to do everything within your power to start changing this downward fall of thoughts to an upward, positive trend. So start today doing your part by trying to make good thoughts a daily habit. Your next step is to explain to your family, relatives, friends, neighbors, and everyone you meet the power and importance of positive thinking. You must become very eager and enthusiastic over your task of spreading good thoughts around. This is necessary to eventually achieve unanimous positive thinking for the world.

In summing up this chapter, we see that God had excellent reasons for wanting to keep Heaven and Earth forever places of positive thought. Your mind-body-spirit unit is put in a state of confusion with the knowledge of both good and evil. It is also adversely affected by the predominant negative thinking of others. Positive thoughts keep your spirits at a high level, while negative thinking brings you down to a low ebb. We can reverse the pull of negative gravity by the means of unanimous positive thinking.

Last but not least, here is an absolute guarantee for your future happiness. So please follow these directions very carefully. Print this indelible sign in your mind's eye, using huge, dark, black letters. It reads: *Danger ahead: negative thoughts. Beware: they are poison. Do not take them into your mind.*

the present day. Throughout the entire Old Testament you will find only a very small minority of positive-thinking people. Notice particularly the predominant adverse thoughts, attitudes, and actions of this era, which produced the bleak environment.

Over nineteen hundred and seventy-three years ago, the promised Savior of the world was born. Christ's entire life was an example of goodness. However, He taught us the most values during the time of His public ministry, which comprised the last three years of His life. He gave us more knowledge in this short period of time than most of us receive in our entire lifetime.

This God-man, Christ, was positive from the very beginning of His life, till the moment He drew His last breath. Nothing daunted His positive attitude, because He was always able to find the hidden benefit in every trial which came His way. So let us start imitating His philosophy of looking for the element of good. Just think, if everyone were willing to try Christ's method for one day, Satan would start losing his negative power over our minds. If we were to continue this unanimous positive effort, Satan's strong influence would be wiped out forever. The world badly needs this positive prescription in order to cure all of her ills.

Christ's life was indeed a living example of positive thinking. He always had the right mental attitude and used the proper mind control for every specific situation. He imbued all of His followers with this same deep conviction of positive belief in good. It enabled them to face up courageously to anything in life without fear, including being devoured by ferocious, hungry lions. Above all, it kept their eyes on the future reward, just as had their Master, who triumphed over a terrible crucifixion and death in order to come to the complete victory of a glorious resurrection.

The Divine Creator possessed an extremely strong belief in the importance of positive thought. You see, He sent His divine Son not only as our Savior, but to reinforce the significance and power of correct thinking. Christ worked a great number of mental and physical miracles to prove this point. He even gave us the precious gift of His own life for our salvation. God wishes us to prepare for our future eternal happiness on Earth. He expects each and every one of you to use your creative mind to make a good, rewarding life for yourself. So the choice of a positive or negative environment is entirely up to you.

Jesus sent His favorite messenger, Mary, back to Earth quite a number of times to tell us how He wanted us to live. On one occasion He even made a personal appearance to a very holy woman in order to make a special devotion well known. However, most of His efforts seem to have been in vain, when we look upon our world of predominant, negative Earthlings. I am sure if Christ decided to have His Second Coming occur today, He would still find the same negativism which rejected Him the first time.

In summing up the important points, we find that your ego is found in your conscious mind and you must be very careful to keep it under control. Satan appealed to our first parents' egos and thereby succeeded in bringing his negative influence to the world. Let us be wise and follow God.

4

Negative Earthlings

Adam and Eve were the first Earthlings exposed to negative thinking, and we still feel their strong downward pull on the gravity of thought today. Just imagine what a delightful paradise Mother Earth would be this very moment if our first parents had settled for a positive world instead of a negative one. Of course, it would be very foolish to go into negative remorse over the past, because we learn a great deal from our mistakes. We should look upon them as blessings in disguise, because they are, indeed, the stepping stones to a bright, positive future.

Satan started Earth's negative trend the day he tricked Eve in the garden of Eden. He continuously pours his poisonous influence of negative thinking upon the world daily. His dirty work is successfully accomplished with ease, merely by appealing to our ego. You see, he makes us feel confident that our bad choices are really very intelligent decisions. Likewise, it is a known fact that Satan convinces many Earthlings of the false and mistaken idea that he never existed at all. Naturally he wants us to believe this lie, because it makes his deceitful job of turning everything good into bad and everything bad into good so much easier without interference.

Our first parents took a heavy loss listening to the evil serpent. He even successfully managed to convince them of their inability to operate their great computer minds. However, God did not take this privilege away from them at all. Their own strong, negative unbelief destroyed this power. Above all, allowing themselves to be overtaken by the devil's deceitful campaign of defeat caused the serious breakdown of their creative minds.

Satan does not really want any Earthling to know the truth about his God-given creative power within. In his own selfish interest, he wants to keep your great ability a deep, dark secret. He realizes your knowledge of this important truth would eventually destroy him and his negative hold on the world. Therefore, he continuously makes an all-out drive to keep this lie alive. For example, if it were possible to take a worldwide pole and ask the question "Is your brain exactly like the Divine Creator's brain?" I am sure only a very sparse number of Earthlings would answer yes.

I sincerely believe Satan started laying his groundwork to destroy the world with negative thinking the day he succeeded in turning Adam and Eve away from God. It is no longer necessary for him to put forth much effort himself, because he has droves of negative people ready, willing, and able to do the job for him. You see, he does not have to get personally involved anymore in world affairs, for he can depend entirely upon negative Earthlings to spread his poisonous, destructive thoughts.

It is difficult to understand why so many highly intelligent Earthlings, without having full knowledge of the true facts, seem so willing to cooperate with this powerful source of evil. Little do they know how much they have already harmed the planet Earth and the future damage which will be inflicted by their perpetual negative attitudes. We have indeed been set back aeons of years in every department of endeavor because of our warped brand of thinking. This definitely kills the bloom and growth of creative minds. Remember, as you think, so you are.

Most Earthlings look with great pride upon the conscious part of their minds, because they consider it to be superior to the subconscious. Some even have the opinion that the subconscious is something to fear, very much like an incontrollable wild animal, while the majority of people believe its chief and only purpose is the involuntary control of many of our bodily functions. Only a very small percentage of Earthlings recognize and appreciate the powerful creative ability of their subconscious mind. The devil is desperately trying to defeat and discourage these daring, intelligent elite who are not afraid to experiment with subconscious, creative ideas. Satan wants to frighten us with his false impression that our subconscious self is evil and very dangerous. Nothing could really be further from the truth. What a pity it is to think of the huge number of Earthlings who are adversely affected by Satan's false propaganda. Due to this incorrect belief, many brilliant minds remain dormant and obsolete for an entire lifetime, without being used properly and productively.

It is true that the conscious part of the mind has a greater degree of intelligence, but we cannot solve our problems or obtain better living conditions by using intelligence alone. It is impossible to use either mind by itself and achieve complete success. For this reason, the Divine Creator insisted that our mind-body-spirit machine work together in perfect harmony. The superior mind is used to give spoken directions to the subconscious. These must be accompanied with a vivid mental picture of the desired results and a positive, expectant attitude of the spirit. Every time you follow this correct formula, your faithful subconscious mind will automatically create a favorable solution to your problem in an unbelievably short period of time.

So let us determine now to do everything possible to stop the power of negative thinkers, who are exercising the wrong kind of influence on our lives. The bad habit of filling the mind with dark thoughts is very destructive to your self-image and self-confidence, and also weakens your will. Worst of all, it causes you to lose your ability to operate your great computer brain. Thus, you are unable to successfully solve your problems and make the necessary positive changes for a happy, rewarding life. How many of you are going to continue to let Satan's negative clay mold your destiny?

Allowing our minds to be conditioned by negative thinking makes us prime targets of self-seekers, who use us chiefly for enriching their own glory and pocketbooks. We are, in reality, treated like puppets who are controlled by the mere pull of a string. Individuals who permit others to take charge of their minds are already dead while still living.

We are constantly being barraged with negative suggestions, and we are very foolish to fall for them hook, line, and sinker, without even so much as checking their validity. This brainwashing takes place every minute of the day. The following is an example of the many negative expectations we are being fed daily. We're told to expect to be old and gray at a certain age, lose our libido in middle life, become overweight, and resign ourselves to a lifetime of rigid dieting, have poor muscle tone, poor eyesight, poor hearing, have bodies racked with pain, lose our productiveness, lose our mental and physical abilities, lose our energy, and above all, lose our zest for living on Earth and our belief in everlasting happiness in the hereafter. Dwelling on unfavorable conditions will actually create them in our lives. You see the subconscious mind immediately acts upon all suggestions, whether they are good or bad. Therefore, your life today is the product of your thoughts of many yesterdays.

The Divine Creator loved us so very much that He gave everyone a brain exactly like His. It must make Him very sad to see the majority of Earthlings failing to use their magnificent minds properly. Our predominant negative thinking has just about reduced us to the level of a bunch of roving robots. Most of us have become hopelessly imprisoned within the negative slots of our minds. We are perfectly content to be automatically programmed whenever the operator decides to press the button. Earthlings take great pride in their intelligence and decision-making abilities. Is it not foolish to allow negative opinions to decide your future?

You could very easily help to defeat the gloomy predictions of Satan's negative thinkers by following God's positive method. You must start filling your mind with good, constructive thoughts now. Then success and happiness will rightfully become your heritage. The secrets of life are locked in the depth of your own marvelous mind. Only there will you find the fountains of youth, health, longevity and success. Your wonderful subconscious friend is ready, willing, and able to create a bright new future for you. Let him get started on the job today.

To sum up, Adam and Eve were the first Earthlings to be exposed to Satan's negative thinking. Thus, Satan is responsible for the predominant negativism of Mother Earth. We can easily reverse Satan's negative tide by using God's power of positive thinking.

5

A Positive Planet Perceived

My subconscious perception tells me that somewhere far beyond the blue there is an unknown planet called Paradise. It is inhabited with human beings exactly like the people of Earth. However, there is one vast difference between the two planets. Earth is predominantly negative, while Paradise is completely positive.

I believe God created Paradise immediately after the fall of Adam and Eve in order to compensate for Earth's failure. No doubt, a virile, handsome, strong-willed man named Esid* was the first Paradisian made in God's image and likeness. Then the Divine Creator decided to make the man a companion out of one of his ribs. So He showed Esid how to deaden his body, by the means of positive suggestion, in order to make the surgery painless. Out of Esid came a beautiful, feminine, strong-willed woman named Para.* Thus, Esid and Para had the honor of being the first people of Paradise.

Satan was extremely jealous of the man and woman living on the new planet Paradise. So he decided to change himself into a serpent again and trick these Paradisians as he did the first Earthlings. After all, Adam and Eve fell for his lie; so it would be easy to deceive these people, too. However, much to Satan's surprise, Para gave him a very cold, unfriendly reception. No matter how hard he tried, he was unable to penetrate her ego. She asked him to leave several times, but

* The names Esid and Para are taken from the word Paradise.

17

he stubbornly refused to do so. He just kept on repeating his negative suggestions, hoping to break down her resistance.

Finally, the evil one thought he was about to win another victory, because he saw the woman go over to the forbidden tree of knowledge. She picked a large, beautiful piece of fruit, but instead of eating it, Para threw it at his head. This made Satan very angry, but he decided to stay anyway. You see, the woman's husband was walking toward them, and the serpent thought he might be able to influence him. Para didn't want Esid to be bothered with Satan's negativism; so she decided it was time to take drastic action to end this unpleasant visit. So she quickly crushed his head with her heel, and the evil serpent went limping away with his hurt pride. Guess you all must be wondering how the first woman of Paradise could resist Satan's temptations so much more easily than the first woman of Earth. You see, Para had a definite advantage over Eve because of her prior knowledge of the Eden incident. Therefore, she was determined not to repeat the same fatal mistake.

Esid and Para loved God very much and were extremely grateful for all His blessings. Most of all, they treasured and revered their great computer minds, likened to God's mind and possessing His creative powers. The Divine Creator was very pleased with their constant expression of good, positive thoughts. Above all, He was proud of their supreme victory over Satan. Therefore, He rewarded them with His promise to keep Paradise for all eternity a positive planet.

So in this delightful, loving, happy atmosphere, Esid and Para increased and multiplied. Para joyfully gave birth to her first son without pain and named him Niac.* The first family of Paradise was very proud of their healthy baby boy. How they wished to have relatives, neighbors and friends to rejoice with them. God heard their fervent prayer and immediately

* The name of Cain spelled backwards becomes Niac.

18

created great numbers of men out of complete nothingness. Then He performed the painless rib surgery on them, in order to give each man a beautiful wife. So it was not very long before the Paradisians had their first population explosion. Esid and Para were exceedingly pleased to have Paradise filled with people. Above all, they were happy that Niac would have playmates. All the Paradisians rejoiced upon hearing the good news that Para had given birth to a second son painlessly. The new baby was named Elba* Niac was very happy to have a little brother.

The happy home life of the first Paradisian family was, indeed, an inspiration to everyone. Esid had the honor of being the head of his family, while Para had the privilege of being the heart of her home. However, they were equal partners in all important decisions and both shared a high level of compatibility. Daily they expressed in words and actions their deep love of God, by loving themselves, each other, their children, and all their relatives, neighbors, and friends. Esid and Para were very wise parents, because they always gave equal approval to both sons and never showed a preference. Therefore, there was no rivalry between the boys, and this enabled them to get along well. These children learned very early in life to appreciate the deep spirit of love, which was practiced in their home.

Niac and Elba, like all other young Paradisians, were given special lessons in the correct use of their great computer minds. They were encouraged to experiment freely with the creative ideas of their choice. The children were taught reading, spelling, writing, and mathematics in the pleasant surroundings of home. This basic education prepared them for self-instruction in many interesting subjects, using their creative abilities. Therefore, the only Paradisians attending college are those seeking degrees for specialized vocations.

* The name Elba is from Abel.

19

As you can see, the youth of Paradise are educated in a positive atmosphere of joy. Unlike Earthlings, they do not depend entirely upon their conscious minds for learning. These wise Paradisians use their God-given computer brains. Therefore, they are not imprisoned for long hours in classrooms and burdened with time-consuming homework. Also, there is an extra bonus for them, because God blesses people for using their special talent by giving them more abilities. No wonder there are so many geniuses in Paradise; every cell in their magnificent minds is charged with productiveness.

The positive thoughts, attitudes, and good example of the Paradisians are quite a contrast to the negativism of most Earthlings. People are indeed the product of the environment in which they grow. Therefore, spirituality, intelligence, abilities, and health are definitely affected by your free choice of a positive or negative way of life. Your great computer brain cannot operate efficiently in a predominantly negative atmosphere. It must be perpetually bathed in the pure water of positive thought in order to reach its highest potential. No matter how positive an Earthling's attitude may become, it will be impossible for him to attain this height of perfection. You see, he has been set back by the dark cloud of negativism which covered Mother Earth early in her infancy. This negative blackout is still visible and continues to cast gloom on our creative powers.

The Paradisians have had the good fortune to live on a positive planet since the very beginning of their existence. They have never had one negative obstacle to block their creative abilities. Therefore, they will always be holier, happier, healthier, and have a greater degree of intelligence than we negative Earthlings, and we will never be able to catch up with them. These people must be aeons of years ahead of us in technology and all other lines of endeavor, because of their unanimous faith, trust, and belief in the power of their great computer minds.

I sincerely believe the Paradisians are the occupants of the

UFOs which are so frequently seen flying in Earth's sky. These colorful, speedy, noiseless spacecraft are, indeed, beyond any spaceship ever built by Earthlings. I also think the Paradisians look exactly like us and are not weird-appearing creatures at all. Likewise, it is my belief that they possess the unique ability to instantly change their appearance, in order to avoid recognition. This same subconscious power can be used to make them invisible, should necessity call for this type of protection. No doubt, all motorized vehicles and electronic equipment can be operated silently for short periods of time, in order to avoid detection. This great feat is temporarily achieved by harnessing energy from the highly developed synchronized electrodes of their great computer brains.

The Paradisians must deeply appreciate their faithful subconscious friend, who is responsible for their extraordinary powers. They can confidently depend on their God within to provide the correct responses for their particular needs. For example, if a Paradisian was trapped in a burning airplane at high altitude, he would not freeze with fear and expect death like an Earthling. He would merely give this expectant command to his subconscious servant: "Wings, please." At that moment his arms would immediately be given the power of wings to fly him to safety. If a Paradisian were a passenger aboard a sinking ship, he would not die of panic. He would simply give this positive direction to his creative mind: "Let the ocean support my weight." He would most assuredly find the immediate means to save his life. I am sure the positive Paradisians use mind power to control many other catastrophic situations.

We, too, could use our great power for self-preservation and protection if we would follow the positive example of Earthlings' Savior, Jesus Christ, the God-man. You see, all of us are made in his image and likeness and possess His omnipotence and omniscience. Christ's tremendous record of miracles and supernatural feats proves His divinity to the

21

world. Recall, particularly, how the amazed apostles saw Jesus walking on the sea without sinking. We could also walk on the ocean without the fear of drowning if we had the strong faith, trust, and belief in our God-mind within.

Thus, it should not be difficult for you to understand the unusual achievements obtained by the Paradisians through mind power. These positive thinking people have always had faith and belief in their creative abilities and have continuously practiced the correct use of their computer minds. Faith, hope, belief, and expectancy are indeed the main ingredients for success. We, too, must strive to acquire these good, positive qualities.

God must have special love for the positive Paradisians, who have chosen to remain His faithful children forever. These good people are most grateful for all of their God-given gifts but particularly appreciate their magnificent, creative minds. Therefore, God continuously showers abundant blessings upon the inhabitants of this peaceful planet of positive good.

You must all be wondering how Paradise must really look. My faithful subconscious friend has clearly perceived this positive planet for me. I have been given a very vivid description, which I am most eager to share with you.

The beautiful, heavenly blue Paradisian sky is breathtaking to behold. Likewise, the soft, green, velvet carpet of weedless grass, which miraculously stays the same length without being cut. What great pleasure, also, to look upon the pure, sparkling bodies of water, which are filled with healthy fish and aquatic life. The air is caressed by the purity of the natural environment, which is, indeed, the breath of life.

The pleasant fragrance from the abundant variety of flowers fills the air, and looking upon their gorgeous, multicolored hue is sheer ecstasy. The large, unusual roses growing on thornless bushes are, indeed, the most outstanding. It is also a delight to see the tremendous crops of healthy vegetables, which are grown in the naturally enriched soil. This protects the plants from the infestation of insects and disease. Likewise, nothing can surpass the splendor of the strong, magestic trees, with their lustrous, thick leaves, which serve as umbrellas of shade. Many are adorned with delicious, sweet varieties of fruit, whose beauty is never marred with insect blemishes. You see, nature works in perfect harmony in this peaceful atmosphere.

The beautiful, indescribable colors of the friendly birds, who are unafraid of people, bring much joy to the planet, singing their delightful, happy songs. All the animals are extremely handsome and very gentle, too. It is not a bit unusual to see a small child petting a lion, tiger, bear, or wolf. Never before have I seen so many outstanding breeds and colors of dogs, cats and horses. These animals seem to possess a higher degree of intelligence than those on Earth. I suppose their positive surroundings must make the difference.

All life on this planet wisely adheres to the laws of nature. Thus, there is no pollution, because the air, water, and land are completely untouched by man's artificiality. Everything is controlled by positive action here. For example, the Paradisian sun performs daily miracles on trash piled high in open bins by changing it into mineral-enriched soil. Solar energy plus many new types of fuel made from nature are used to power Paradise.

The magnificent homes and buildings equipped with modern conveniences unheard of on Earth are indeed masterpieces of advanced architecture. Likewise, the superb design and advancement in the mechanical and electrical technology of land, sea, air, and outer space motorized vehicles is beyond the wildest dream of every Earthling engineer. All the materials used in manufacturing the needs of this positive planet come directly from natural resources.

The Paradisian climate is indeed miraculous, because the temperature forever remains perfect. However, the people can equally enjoy both summer and winter sports every day.

——— 6 ———

Your Positive Response

No doubt there are mixed feelings regarding your personal response to the positive planet, Paradise. Perhaps most of you will follow the negative pattern of grieving over the Earth's loss, which was caused by Adam and Eve's poor choice, while only a very small minority of positive thinkers will take immediate steps to start changing their negative environment to positive.

You, as a dedicated individual, must start your positive response in active motion now. Remember, the power is within each and every one of you to make Mother Earth a much better planet. So you must begin this very moment to weed out all of your negative thoughts, words, actions, and responses and replace them with the positive.

Your goal will be attained much sooner if you have a very vivid picture of a positive response imprinted in your mind's eye. Why not use the purity of a waterfall as your motto of positive good. Just listening to the soothing sound of the steady flow of water eases your tensions, exactly as good thoughts and attitudes bring peace to your mind. You know, a watergate is used to keep out destructive flood waters. So you must use your own mental watergate to stop negative thoughts, attitudes, and responses from entering your mind.

The next important step is an honest self-analysis of the reasons for your present negative response to life. This valuable information will help you to eliminate the problem. Remember, your past mistakes must be looked upon as the stepping stones to your bright, successful future. You always derive some positive good from every failure. Therefore, it is entirely up to you to condition your mind to give positive responses to them.

The very best place to begin your positive movement is right in your own home. You will have the golden opportunity to practice on a variety of different personalities of various ages. Thus, you'll obtain an excellent education on the benefits of handling people in a positive manner. This will prepare you well indeed for your apostolate of positive response to the negative world.

Those of you who are fortunate enough to have a newborn baby or very young children in your family will be able to observe the best example of positive response. You see, all babies come into this world imbued with a very high level of the positive spirit. They are, indeed, natural born positive thinkers, because this is the will of the Divine Creator. However, by the time these children reach school age, they have already been conditioned to respond negatively to the world. So it is up to us to help reverse this response to positive.

Little children naturally take to the positive, very much like young ducklings take to water. Enthusiastic youngsters of all ages can teach us a great deal about the merits of positive thinking. Just image how much happier and harmonious our homes would be if we adults agreed to become God's trusting spiritual children again. Then we could easily start flowing freely along with His good tide of positivism. Saturating our minds with good thoughts enables us to give our children daily examples of the proper positive responses to everyday living. Soon they will be imitating their parents, by actively carrying out their own personal positive responses to life. Therefore, being conditioned to respond in a positive manner early in childhood prepares these children to become tomorrow's positive-minded adults. Their minds will be filled with God's power of positivism, which will eventually overcome and eliminate Satan's negative, evil influence in the world. Mother Earth needs positive direction and leadership in every one of her beloved countries. So it is the important responsibility of every parent to start at the cradle, nurturing the spirit of positivism.

Why not decide this very moment to start bringing your personal, enthusiastic positive response to your own home. You see, Satan's negativism is desperately trying to destroy the earth's beautiful family tradition. So you can help defeat his evil plan by beginning now to change your present negative home environment to a positive one. Your job will be accomplished in an amazingly short period of time by faithfully applying the Golden Rule in your life. You'll always be a winner, using this tried and proven method to achieve a loving relationship with every member of your family.

Jews and Christians alike can cling steadfastly to this rock of truth in Matthew, Chapter 7, verse 12: "Therefore all that you wish men to do to you, even so do you also to them; for this is the Law and the Prophets." These brief statements are the teachings of the law of Moses in a nutshell. I am sure even atheists and agnostics can understand and appreciate the logic of this philosophy. Applying these positive words of God's wisdom in your daily living will not only bring you personal peace, but will also bring God's treasure of lasting peace to your home. Your family can quickly speed its desired goal of unity and harmony by frequently repeating together, "Do unto others as you would have others do unto you." However, the father, mother, and each child must personally take the responsibility of consciously imprinting this message of peace upon his own mind. Then your marvelous subconscious friend will create an ideal, friendly, loving relationship within your family circle.

People living in a home using the Golden Rule as their motto will have a definite advantage over those living in a negative atmosphere. No matter how much trouble is going on in the outside world, they can always look forward to returning to the peace and security of their God-oriented homes. Remember, "Where two or more are gathered together in My name, there I am in the midst of them" (Matthew 18:20). So your family can always be assured of the continuous living presence of the Prince of Peace. He will forever shut out Satan's negativism so that every member of your family can joyfully live as His spiritual child. Hold fast to the Golden Rule, because it is the key to a happy home.

So do not hesitate another moment to start faithfully practicing the Golden Rule in your home. I absolutely guarantee these simple positive words of love will make a miraculous change in your present family climate. They will automatically turn on the positive virtues of love, faith, hope, kindness, patience, understanding, trust, meekness, mildness, humbleness, and purity of heart. Making the Golden Rule come alive through your personal actions will make these words of Holy Scripture "Be ye perfect as your Heavenly Father is perfect" a living reality. You see, you will be definitely expressing life as God's spiritual child through your dynamic positive response to His Holy Words.

It is quite natural for you to want to share this effective method with others, upon seeing the good results obtained in your own home. Therefore, you will become most eager to bring your positive spirit of response to everyone. So remember to take it with you wherever you may go. Take it to church, to work, to school, to hospitals, to business, to management, to labor, to play, to sports and to all recreational and social activities. Above all, bring your positive response to sickness, death, and all the many other unpleasant situations of life. You must take the personal responsibility for bringing it to all of your relatives, friends, and enemies, too. Next, you must dedicate yourself to the task of bringing it to clergymen, religious orders, teachers, national, state, civic and local leaders, doctors, dentists, nurses, lawyers, all officers of the law, the sales profession, the military, servants, and all employed Earthlings. Your enthusiastic efforts of positive response will greatly enrich the negative world.

Your positive response of good will not only help to make Mother Earth a better planet, but will also give you the added bonus of many extra personal rewards. For example, you will always be holier, healthier, happier, younger, more successful, and be surrounded by an abundance of loving people. You see, the magnetism of your positive thoughts, attitudes, and responses toward life automatically draws all the good of Heaven and Earth back to you. So do not let another day pass without bringing the joy of your positive responses to the troubled world.

To sum up, only a small minority of Earthlings will have a positive response to the planet Paradise. You should be determined to start the immediate action of your own personal response.

The reason for your predominant negativism will be found deep within yourself. You can quickly overcome it by the effective means of your positive response.

It is extremely important for you to bring your personal enthusiastic response to your family. This will help to overcome Satan's evil scheme. Faithfully practicing the Golden Rule in our homes will destroy the negative spirit. The families of Earth will eventually achieve a supreme victory over Satan.

It is the sacred duty of every dedicated Earthling to bring his positive response to the troubled world.

——7——

Let Your Positive Light Shine

Your continuous, enthusiastic positive response will definitely ignite the spark of God's life within you. This enkindled light of His love and hope will be visible in your eyes, while Satan's negative responses only reflect his evil darkness. May I quote from the Gospel according to St. Matthew, chapter 6, verses 22 and 23: "The lamp of the body is the eye: therefore if thine eye be single, thy whole body shall be full of light: But if thine eye be evil, thy whole body shall be full of darkness . . . how great is that darkness!" Therefore, your eyes are indeed the windows of your soul. They either express your positive good or your dark negativism to the world. Good thoughts, attitudes, desires, and responses turn on your brilliant personal beam of light, which safely guides you down the path of life, while bad, destructive thoughts, attitudes, desires, and responses turn it off and cause you to fall down into your own evil abyss of negative darkness. Thus, the free choice of God's light or Satan's darkness is entirely up to you. So why not decide this very moment to let your positive light shine.

The first important step is to focus your mind's eye on the future target of success. Then, actually see yourself using a huge, red broom to sweep out all of your negative, corruptive, poisonous thoughts. This mental housecleaning is as beneficial to your mind as a spring tonic is to your body. It is most necessary for your mind, body, and spirit to be continuously washed in the fountain of pure thoughts, in order to project the brilliant light of God's positive good. Your sparkling, alive eyes filled with God's love will definitely improve your appearance. Likewise, it will improve your

31

outlook on life and will succeed in lifting the spirits of everyone around you. Above all, your personal spark of hope will eventually help to turn on God's light in Satan's darkened, negative world. So let us try to get as many volunteers as possible to shine their positive lights.

You will soon find how important and necessary it is for you to start shining your positive light. Keenly observing the expressions in most people's eyes around you will definitely cause you to take positive steps to bring your personal ray of hope to them. Sad to say, but the majority of eyes reveal anxiety, uneasiness, trouble, sadness, pain, and sorrow, while only a very small minority of eyes express God's treasure of peace, joy, and contentment. These people most certainly have their share of problems and troubles, too. How can they manage so cleverly to keep the telltale signs out of their eyes? You see, they have learned the secret art of melting adversities away with God's sunshine of positive good. Their God light from within shines brilliantly on every misfortune. It immediately finds the tiny speck of positive good in it. Therefore, they always have something left to build on for the future. Thus, the darkest situation in life will never stop their positive lights from shining. I sincerely hope all of you will soon be lighting the negative world with your positive glow, too.

I am sure many of you will feel it is impossible to shine your own positive light. Your life at the present moment may be so burdened with sorrow and suffering that there seems to be no way out of your utter hopelessness. Fortunately, you can depend upon the shining lights of others to help lead you out of your negative prison. However, you must eventually be prepared to shine your personal light on your gloomy mental world in order to attain a complete victory. Remember, positive thinking is the powerful current of energy which switches on your brilliant glow. Therefore, you have everything within you to do the job. So why not get started now.

Of course, my heart goes out to those of you who have a

severe health problem or serious illness in your family. The death of a loved one is indeed about the most difficult blow one encounters in life. However, worst of all is the loss of the love, respect, admiration, and affection of a cherished person who is still very much alive. Nothing can compare to the suffering and heartache associated with an endeared one being dead to you while still living. Take for example the plight of a divorcé, who is still very much in love with his former mate. The suffering of children whose happy home has been broken up due to divorce. The torture of a divorced parent, who has had his children turned against him. The horror of knowing your child is being treated unjustly by his stepmother or stepfather. The grief-stricken parents, whose discontented, unhappy teenager has left home forever or has become a drug addict. The anguish of parents being deprived of seeing one of their grown children, because of the unreasonable demands of the son's or daughter's spouse. The agony of a faithful son or daughter who has been cut off from a beloved parent, due to the poisonous influence of the mother's or father's second spouse or some other close member of the immediate family. The heartache and loneliness of senior citizens who have been abandoned by their children and relatives. No matter how deadly and terrifying the above situations may appear to you, I guarantee your positive light will be able to melt each and every one of them away. You see, I have been blessed with having the personal, practical experience of living with one of these ugly situations for almost two years. Therefore, I can vouch for your success in using this positive method to build a brand-new, exciting life for yourself.

It is of the utmost importance to fill the trauma of your mind with God's positive light. This will enable you to express His warmth and goodness to those around you, despite your present, adverse circumstances. You also must mentally shine your God light on the lost love of your life. Your continuous, magnetic glow will eventually enkindle the spark of hope, which might possibly unite you once again with your beloved. It may take days, months or years to attain success. One thing for sure, you will certainly develop the virtue of fortitude in the process. However, I must warn you about a possible pitfall your positive light might encounter. You must be prepared for the painful prospect of your perpetual shine failing to lead your endeared one back to you. It is most necessary for you to face the fact that he may never return to his former status. Likewise, he may even continue his un-friendly spirit for the duration of his life. Please do not allow this negative possibility to darken your future. You can always count on your faithful positive light. It will immedi-ately find God's ray of sunshine in every unpleasant out-come. You see, someday you will be enjoying complete happiness with this special person in the next world. You can be sure, no one will have the power to keep you apart in God's home of perfect peace. Remember, all the ugly situa-tions encountered on this negative Earth become beautiful in the positive atmosphere of Heaven.

Your positive light is never wasted in vain, even if it did not have enough power to change your adverse condition or renew your close, personal relationship. The continuance of your patient, persistent glow is sure to bring the reward of some new, favorable circumstance or another special some-one into your life. Your brilliant shine is bound to eventually send back the bright reflection of positive good. This is one of the many important laws of nature which you will quite happily wish to obey. Remember, you only reap the harvest of what you actually sow in your own life. So let us make all our seeds positive ones.

The tide of life is a forever changing one. Supernatural life is the only exception to this rule. Almighty God steadfastly remains the one and same unchanging person forever and ever. However, all other living matter is continuously moving forward to a more advanced, mature stage. We are constantly being subjected to this very wise law of our Creator, in order to reach fulfillment and to prevent stagnation. If you become rebellious, stubborn, or lazy, and refuse to flow along freely with Mother Nature's cycle of never-ending renewal, an unexpected roadblock will most assuredly alter your course. Then you will be forced into moving in a different direction. You could have easily avoided a great deal of unnecessary delays and disappointments by permitting your positive light to guide you safely down life's path. Its brilliant beam would have detected every one of your detours ahead of time. This would have enabled you to wisely prepare in advance for them. Your Beloved Creator gave you the means to create the necessary good changes in your life. He wanted so very much to save you from the painful metamorphosis of negative thinking. So start following your guiding light of positive thought today. You will be rewarded with your continuous rebirth to a new, refreshing life.

The persistent projection of your shining light will help a great many people to become reborn in the spirit of positive good. This will be accomplished by urging others to light their own positive lamps. Then they, also, will be able to bring sunshine to the garden of their minds. This will make them come alive with the fertility and youth of positive thinking. So always share your delightful, positive glow with others. You will find it very contagious, and it will not be long before everyone will be catching it. Your glorious radiance acts like a powerful ray, giving out all of God's positive good to the troubled world. What a great pleasure to look into sparkling, bright eyes filled with God's love! How can you honestly say that you cannot see God today? Every moment His image is reflected through the positive shine of your glowing eyes. Remember, you must fill the camera of your mind with the superior film of positive thinking in order to take a lifelike picture of Him. I sincerely hope all of you will want to become one of God's professional photographers very soon.

The warmth of your personal glow will indeed help to

ignite the spark of hope for God's positive light in the negative world. There is always strength in numbers. So it is your responsibility to encourage as many people as possible to let their positive light shine. Your most powerful drawing card will be your own good example as an active positive thinker. Therefore, you must go out on the highways and byways and invite your fellowmen to the important banquet of positive thinking. The friendly beam of your shining light will certainly entice everyone to come along with you. So bring as many guests as possible, because great numbers of positive lamplighters are needed very badly. Your future reward will be seeing the multitude of brilliant personal lamps turning on the unanimous good of Christ, the light of the world. Is this goal not a worthwhile cause for you? So do not wait until tomorrow to let your positive light shine—do it today.

To sum up, your eyes reveal your predominantly positive or negative spirit. They either reflect God's positive light or Satan's negative darkness. You alone have the freedom to choose. However, your mind must be filled with an abundance of good, positive thoughts in order to light your own brilliant, personal lamp. God's image, love, and energizing life is brought to the world by you. The camera of your mind accomplishes this miracle every time you let your positive light shine.

Your God light will bring sunshine to your adversities. It will find the thread of hope with which to build a new future. Many volunteers are needed to shine their positive lights on Satan's negativism. Establishing God's permanent light in the world will be our supreme victory. So start this moment to shine your positive light and never turn it off.

8

Meet the Big You Within

The perpetual shining of your positive light will lead you down the path to one of life's greatest discoveries. Its brilliant beam will penetrate deep inside you. There you will find the secret treasure that has been locked in your mind for an entire lifetime. So with great pleasure, I would like you to meet the big you within. You will immediately recognize him to be your marvelous subconscious friend. He has been working as your faithful servant ever since the day you took your first breath of life. Every one of you will soon find him to be indispensable, in regard to your good health and happiness. No matter how many years you have lived on Earth, it is never too late to become acquainted with him. Of course, the sooner you get to know him, the better will be your life.

You need your big you in your life much more than he needs you. Without his help, you will never be able to reach your highest potential. No matter how brilliant and intelligent you may be, it will still take double the time to accomplish your goal by using your conscious media alone. Remember, your big you has the priority on creativity and instant action. These qualities are very necessary to bring a successful job to a speedy conclusion. Many worthwhile projects are foolishly discontinued because of impatience, frustration, and disappointment over not obtaining quick enough results. Very often your success was just around the next corner, but your stubborn refusal to follow your big you's positive light of keen insight doomed you to failure. Just think, you could easily have been a whiz-bang success had you put your big you in full command of the situation.

So why continue any longer using your present, conscious, halfway measures alone to pilot your personal ship of life? Just making your big you the captain will make the rest of the voyage so much smoother. So do not wait until tomorrow; put your big you in charge today.

Many of you are struggling to climb the ladder of success in your chosen career. You all know the definite advantage of being in good standing with the big wheel of your company. You will soon find that it pays to be on friendly terms with him and to have your best foot forward at all times. His personal evaluation of you counts more toward your future promotion than your intelligence, special abilities, and workmanship. This same healthy attitude, likewise, applies to your big you within, who is really the big wheel of your mind. Remember, he has the power to spin you any direction that you really want to go. All you must tell him is when, where, what, and why and he will automatically produce the know-how in an unbelievably short period of time. So you can see it is entirely up to you to consciously call your own winning signals. You must choose whether you want to get started on your mission in low or high gear. Only you can decide the takeoff time, destination, and the expected time of arrival. Remember, you are always consciously in the driver's seat and your big you's motor will faithfully obey your speed limits. So will you go full speed ahead or do you plan to be slowed down by many unnecessary negative stops and starts? Your positive words are the inexpensive fuel which powers your big you's engine. You are the important person who sets the pace. So please give him your road map of clear, positive directions now. This will enable you to get started immediately on your new, exciting, successful adventure.

Your big you is also your faithful lifetime protector. Look upon him as being the guardian angel of your mind and body. Just think, he spends his entire life operating all of your organs and glands, without one wink of sleep. He always hears every one of your calls and is immediately ready to respond to them with the proper, positive action. He desperately wants to take you by the hand and lead you safely down life's path with his love, protection, and guidance. You would save yourself a great deal of worries, mishaps, and miseries by allowing him to do his job without your negative interference. What a pity, to think about those of you who do not even know or appreciate your big you. I personally believe he is the spirit of God living within you. He is that very special, unique, invisible, good part of you which is made in God's image and likeness. Your big you within is, likewise, omnipotent, omniscient, and immortal. However, these extraordinary powers are meaningless unless you consciously direct him to use them. Only with his positive current of good can you remove the mountainous obstacles of negativism and finally gain tremendous positive heights. Entrust your future to your big you today and you will soon be able to make a new and better tomorrow for yourself and your loved ones.

Nothing hurts your big you more than remaining a dormant prisoner, deprived of his creativity. You personally impose this unfair sentence upon him by your continuous, stubborn refusal to recognize and appreciate his special abilities. It annoys him to see you struggle and stumble through life without his creative power. Your urgent call for his help could easily have turned the negative tide in your favor. So it would be well for all of you to look upon your big you within as one of the most important parts of your mind-body-spirit machine. You will soon find your friendly approval and your humble acknowledgment of your dependence upon your big you will start paying off with big, positive dividends. Remember, the humble are always the first ones to be served at the banquet table of life. Therefore, your humble, appreciative, positive, expectant attitude regarding your big you is extremely important for your future. You see, it automatically guarantees you his prime service for

would never want to do anything to stop him from working in your favor. Your big you's power is harnessed with the magnetism of your positive thoughts and words. Therefore, you must remember to accentuate the positive and eliminate the negative in order to avoid a bad trip. Whenever your life turns sour and the bottom seems to drop out of everything, your conscious mind is solely responsible for the trouble. The adverse condition or setback occurs due to your faulty instructions to your big you within. You see, he never fails to respond to any of your positive or negative requests. Therefore, you must be extremely careful with your choice of thoughts and words. They can either bring you happiness or misery. Remember, the decision is always your conscious one. So why not become a habitual, positive thinker. Then you will never have to worry any more about unpleasant reversals.

Despite the great regard you and I may have for the big you within, we must try to understand the reason why some people have such a low opinion of him. I personally think it is due to the mistaken belief that many physical, mental, and emotional problems originate in the subconscious mind. Little do they know that conscious negativism is actually the root of the trouble. The subconscious is triggered into perpetuating the unfavorable condition by our continuous negative suggestions and actions. Sometimes the original source of the difficulty remains subconsciously hidden for an entire lifetime. Therefore, health can only be restored by consciously removing the cause.

Another very important point to remember is the fact that the subconscious mind cannot rationalize or analyze. It depends entirely on conscious energy for stimulation. Therefore, any bad condition existing in your creative mind is the direct result of your negative thoughts, words, and responses. Can you not see that your big you within is definitely not the culprit? The trouble is always due to your incorrect, negative signals. So why not make a fresh start today for a new future by turning the negative side of your life's record over to the positive side.

Do you remember how the devil serpent in the garden of Eden persuaded our first parents to believe they had forever lost the ability to use their great computer minds? Down through the ages we have erroneously continued to follow this negative pattern, without making a thorough investigation. For this reason, most Earthlings look upon their big you within as a personal devil instead of an angel of mercy. Therefore, it is the sacred duty of each and every one of you to become apostles of the truth for the positive purpose of blotting out Satan's vicious lie. Every Earthling must hear the good news, that he can make a better world for himself and his fellowmen with the magic of positive thinking. Let us wise up to the fact that we all have the conscious means to generate our creative minds. However, it is most necessary for everyone to know the correct way to use it. This vital message must be brought to every corner of the Earth. The very best example you can give to the predominant negative world is your own superb, conscious control of your big you within. I guarantee this kind of effective advertising will sell droves of people on the benefits of positive thinking.

To sum up, we will continue to have misery and deplorable conditions in the world until every Earthling meets his big you within. Above all, we must learn to use the secret formula of good thoughts, words, and responses. Remember, this is the powerful fuel which gyrates the creative mind into positive action. A good trip can only be attained by keeping your big you on a positive course. This will bring you the happy landing of lasting, successful achievements. However, you will be extremely surprised to learn that there are some rare occasions when it will be to your decided advantage to take a reverse trip with your big you. You can eagerly look forward to reading the explanation for this seemingly negative action in the next chapter.

Each and every one of you possesses a marvelous instrument within, which has the power to bring you a new, exciting way of life. You can always keep it in perfect tune by avoiding the negative off-key status. So, with this refreshing thought in mind, I challenge you to start practicing your positive notes today. I promise your positive music will turn the sunshine on your present dark clouds. Your big you within is most eager to take you on an exciting trip. He is ready, willing, and able to take off any time. He is patiently awaiting your go-ahead signal. Please shine the green light for him now. I guarantee it will be the most thrilling trip of your entire life.

9

Take a Subconscious Trip

One of the most exhilarating, exciting adventures you can experience is to take a subconscious trip. I guarantee this supreme ecstasy will thrill you beyond your wildest dreams. You will feel as if you are on cloud number seven on your way to heaven. How lucky you are to have a personal pilot who is ready at a moment's notice to take you away from it all. Just simply tell him where you want to go and what you wish to see. He will provide immediate transportation accompanied with vivid description.

Your marvelous subconscious mind remembers everything that has occurred in your life from the moment of your conception. He can even take you back to the period of your prenatal life. I am sure most of you will wholeheartedly agree that it is a positive action to go forward and a negative one to go backward. However, you will find there are certain times when it will definitely prove advantageous to take a reverse subconscious trip. For example, you may have an illness which your doctor believes to be caused by a hidden culprit in your past. Maybe you are suffering from extreme fears, nervousness, anxieties, or lack of self-confidence. You may be fighting the battle of obesity, excessive dependence upon drugs, or desperately trying to overcome some other bad habit. Perhaps you are allowing yourself to be mentally tormented over an unknown fact relating to your early life for the above reasons or any other unresolved, negative situation, I highly recommend a reverse subconscious trip. Your big you will take you for a return flight over your past. You can count on his keen radar to detect the origin of your problem. I promise it will turn out to be the most positive trip of your life. Knowing the cause of your trouble will definitely enable you to take immediate positive steps to eliminate it. This will give you and all of your loved ones supreme happiness.

You have the choice of two different routes for a RS trip. If you wish to go at a slower pace, just simply state your problem audibly and confidently expect your pilot to direct you to the cause. Repeat the above instructions often during the day and frequently see a cheerful picture of yourself in your mind's eye free from your present unhappiness. Eventually your subconscious will find your trouble-shooter and every atom of your being will start rejecting it. You can eagerly look forward to your future happy landing, which will indeed be the turning point of your life. Then it will be easy for you to make a fresh start minus your former burden.

However, if you are in a big hurry for your answer, I suggest you take a direct flight over your past. This will enable your subconscious pilot to immediately televise the information back to you. You will no longer have to wonder about your past history, because you can get a flashback of any previous incident by taking a RS TV trip. In order to be successful using this shorter method, it is necessary for you to achieve the complete relaxation of your mind-body-spirit machine. This must be practiced daily, until you are entirely free from tension. Then you will be perfectly prepared for your fascinating, televised RS trip. Just make sure you are in a quiet place, alone, calm, relaxed and confident before takeoff time. Get yourself in a comfortable position near your favorite TV screen and mentally turn on your subconscious channel. Clearly specify the information you wish to be projected and confidently expect a quick reception. Soon you will have the thrilling experience of seeing the scene from your past miraculously appear on your blank TV through the media of subconscious perception. Reliving this part of your life for a few minutes will help you to understand the reason for your present unreasonable, negative response. Above all, it will enable you to effectively change your incorrect, false reaction to a positive one. Therefore, your RS TV trip will turn out to be one of the most forward, rewarding trips you have ever taken. You see, it has put you on the positive track of life. So take as many reverse subconscious trips as are necessary to root out all of your negative darkness.

However, in this predominantly negative world, you will only find a small minority of positive thinkers who believe they can consciously direct the subconscious to turn on their personal life television. I never realized I had this capability myself until I read Dr. Alfred J. Cantor's book entitled *Unitrol.* I heartily recommend you to read this excellent book, too. I took my first reverse, subconscious TV trip on January 29, 1974, in order to clear up a matter involving my early life. Shortly before the picture from my past was shown on the TV screen and also during the reception period, there was a gorgeous aura all about the favorite family chair. This breathtaking sight appeared like brilliant puffs of smoke, very much like a vision. I believe this phenomenon was the result of the electronic energy emanating from my computer brain, which the subconscious used for televising. It was, indeed, an indescribable moment of supreme ecstasy for me. I never dreamed that it was possible for an ordinary person like myself to turn on her own personal TV. However, I must admit my picture was a little bit fuzzy. It would have been much clearer if I had achieved a greater degree of relaxation. I am very pleased with the positive results of this wonderful experience. You see, the doubt concerning my past no longer troubles me anymore, since I took my RS TV trip to face the truth. Each and every one of you can remove any troublesome enemy from your past by taking the reverse subconscious trip of your choice. Remember, you have the power within you to do the job. So make your reservation flight with your subconscious pilot today.

I am sure you will be greatly relieved to learn that it is impossible for an outsider to televise information from your mind. You only have sufficient power on your subconscious channel to receive pictures relating to your own life. Each and every one of you possesses a built-in device which serves to protect you against the invasion of your privacy. You see, the Divine Creator very wisely programmed each individual's subconscious mind to record and verify facts pertaining exclusively to him. Your big you within will only reveal them to you upon your special request. Remember, you are always his chief interest, because you are his entire world. Is it not a great comfort to know that no one else can televise your past life? Your personal secrets forever remain your untouchable property, unless you decide to consciously make them public. However, you must be aware that the subconscious mind of your Divine Creator possesses a supernatural, sensory, perceptive channel that has the extraordinary power to receive and televise every individual's thoughts, words, and actions in the entire universe. He is the only person besides yourself who has access rights to the contents of your mind.

It is my sincere belief that doctors and scientists will soon investigate subconscious perception in its entirety. They will discover many new and unheard-of techniques, which will greatly benefit the sick world. Particularly, I foresee a tremendous positive breakthrough for suffering mankind. Doctors of the future will use reverse subconscious trips as one of their most valuable diagnostic instruments. It will be expecially useful in the treatment of certain diseases, for which medical science is still looking for a proven cure. Tomorrow's doctors will realize the importance of educating and training their patients to communicate with their subconscious pilots. They will spend a great deal of time preparing them to achieve a successful RS trip, in order to detect the original source of their illness. Their subconscious will be able to find quickly the starting point of poor health. He will also show and reveal the lack or overabundance of specific elements which have caused the breakdown. The patient will immediately relate this confidential information to his doctor. Then the doctor will know exactly what to do in order to restore this person to perfect health. The sick patient could very easily speed his recovery and, likewise, help his doctor by the frequent visualization of his advanced cure. He should also constantly urge his personal pilot to either stop or start production of the identified chemicals. I suppose this type of medical treatment sounds too far-out for most of you. However, I fully expect it to be the in thing in the twenty-first century.

Having a personal rendezvous with your future provides another exciting, interesting scenic flight. You can easily achieve this great pleasure by taking a forward trip with your subconscious pilot. It is possible for you to get away any minute of the day. Making your advanced reservation is the only requirement. You will soon find FS trips are exceedingly beneficial to your well-being. Your personal pilot has the unique ability to bring out the hidden beauty in your world. His deep insight will allow you to see life in an entirely new prospective. It will seem like everything is just starting to come alive for the first time. He will definitely give you a fresh, new, enthusiastic outlook on life. This refreshing change will keep you perpetually charged with youthful energy. It will enable you to become one of the beautiful people.

Do you remember when you were a little child how much fun it was to daydream? I am sure all of you still enjoy throwing pennies in a wishing well and blowing out candles on your birthday cakes and making special wishes. It is perfectly delightful to think about a fairy godmother touching you with her magic wand to give you your heart's desires, or a magic carpet that can transport you on a moment's notice to the land of fantasy. However, from this day forward, you will never have to amuse yourself with the world of pretend. You may not have ever been aware of it before, but you really have your very own personal genie within you. He has the power to turn your burning desires into living realities.

All he needs is the fuel of your positive thoughts and words and your conscious imagination for a fast takeoff flight to your brand-new future.

I know all of you will immediately recognize your newly discovered genie to be your marvelous subconscious mind. Every Earthling possesses this superb device. However, only a very small percentage of the world's population perceive their priceless possession and fully understand how to correctly use it. Your personal genie's magic will enable you to overcome all unpleasant situations and effectively tune out obnoxious people. Above all, turn to him for the means of controlling the blues and blahs of your life, instead of consciously copping out with harmful, habit-forming drugs, medications, and excessive dependence upon alcoholic beverages and tobacco. Remember, your personal genie has the creative power to turn bad into good. However, in order for him to do an efficient job, you must be sure to give him clear, concise, positive directions. They must be accompanied with frequent mental pictures of the desired want plus a high spirit of expectancy. Let your imagination run wild and see yourself actually living in a happy land, free from your negative destructive self. In an amazingly short period of time, your daily FS trips to your future life will start paying off. Very soon you will become the free-spirited person that you have always wanted to be, thanks to the magical influence of your wonderful genie within. What do you want or what kind of person do you wish to be? Just ask your personal genie and he will give it to you free. How about going to sleep with this positive thought tonight. I guarantee you will start becoming a new, positive-minded person in the morning.

Your personal genie can also eliminate the many negative hang-ups which most Earthlings have been conditioned to accept as gospel truth. For example, very few people think it is possible for them to escape the shackle of old age. At a certain time of life, most of us automatically expect excessive wrinkles, gray hair, poor posture, and the loss of muscle tone, libido, and productiveness. Many good husbands and wives sincerely believe that their sexual pleasures magically shut off at middle age. They will indeed be greatly surprised to learn that the Divine Creator intended for married couples to enjoy this supreme ecstasy for their entire lifetime. Remember, it is not your chronological age that brands you as an old man or woman. It is your perpetual negative thoughts, attitudes and responses that place you in this antiquated category. You have been endowed with the great gift of free will; so it is entirely up to you to choose your way of thinking. Your good, positive thoughts enable your personal genie to keep you eternally young in spirit and forever sexually desirable to your wife or husband, while your continuous negative thinking encourages your genie to turn on the process of decrepit aging and make youth, buoyancy, and physical attractiveness only past memories. Are you going to continue to follow the herd of negative thinkers or have you decided to let your individual sparkle of positivism make you stand out in the crowd? Remember, the choice is always yours.

Absolutely nothing can compare in beauty and lusciousness to tree-ripened fruit, full-grown vegetables, flowers in full bloom, and tall, majestic trees that have reached their supreme pinnacle of growth. Maturity seems to bring an unsurpassed quality of beauty and elegance in every species of nature. Human beings are no exception to this rule. Mother Nature's entire kingdom responds in a positive manner to maturity and rejoices in its fulfillment. However, man is the only member of the world's living family who frowns disapprovingly on this high peak of his development. He very negatively refers to this stage in his life as old age. Maturity is actually one of the most enjoyable periods of life. It makes you calm, mellow, tender, wise, and lovable. Therefore, eagerly welcome your completion and you will forever kill the negative fear of old age.

How happy it makes me to know that I have helped you to find the wonderful treasure buried deep within you. I am sure you are convinced that your personal genie is everything you have ever wanted all wrapped up in one. Remember, he has the power to put you on the road of rewarding, successful, confident living. His positive magic is indeed your eternal fountain of youth. He can calm your nerves, relax your muscles, overcome your fears, alleviate and deaden your pains. Look upon your special genie as your youth pill, beauty pill, mood pill, nerve pill, sleeping pill, and pain pill. He is also your cop-out drugs, tranquilizers, anesthesia, alcoholic drinks, and your favorite tobacco product. Let him start working his positive magic on you while you sleep tonight. I guarantee you will wake up tomorrow to a brand-new wonderful world of positive living. Continue to feed your personal genie positive thoughts every moment of your life. This is my prescription for your lifetime of happiness.

To sum up, make an immediate reservation with your personal pilot to take a subconscious trip. You have the choice of either going in a forward or a backward direction. You will find both flights to be fascinating experiences. Reverse subconscious trips help you to detect and eliminate negative problems which have their origin in your past. During a reverse flight, it is even possible for your pilot to televise the information back to you. Forward subconscious trips enable you to become a new person in the future and can also create dramatic good changes in your life. Likewise, they can remove negative hang-ups, drug addiction, and other bad habits.

Look upon your subconscious genie as your personal fountain of youth, health, beauty, longevity, and as your creative genius. Continue to turn on his magic with your conscious positivism and I promise you will live a happy life forever and ever.

—10—

Earth's Return to the Positive

What a fantastic place the earth will be the day it returns to the positive. It will be necessary to banish negative thoughts, words, and responses from everyone's mind in order to win this glorious victory. At the moment, this idea may seem like an impossible dream to most of you. However, I fully expect us to accomplish the job in the very near future. You can hasten the moment of this great achievement by continuously keeping your personal world a positive place. You can be sure, the magnetism of your positivism will certainly attract those around you. Gradually you will see the earth's worm of negativism turn over to the positive side. Your powerful, good thoughts will most definitely influence the change of position. Remember, your positive enthusiasm is not only responsible for making you a much better individual, but it also makes the whole world a better place. The splendid example of your own happy, rewarding life is indeed the best bait you can use to convert others to your brand of thinking. Your living advertisement of positivism will encourage others to change their thought patterns, too.

No matter how negative the outside world may appear to you, your personal positivism always keeps your inside world charged with vitality. It enables you to become a happy individual, who lives to enjoy the present moment, never looking back to the past or fearing the future. Look upon positive thinking as a magic wand that can turn you into the free-spirited, open-minded person your Divine Creator intended you to be. You will feel like you are forever flowing in forward motion, perfectly relaxed, contented, at peace with yourself and the world. Perfect balance of mind, body, and spirit will be your positive reward. It will keep you in excellent tune with the whole symphony of nature and in complete harmony with the entire universe. The part of you made in God's image and likeness can now reach out beyond your body to tap the treasures of Heaven and Earth. However, to accomplish this great feat, you must be imbued with the spirit of positive thinking.

So saturate your mind with the perpetual spirit of positivism. Joyfully reflect your personal benefits to the negative world. Frequently have your subconscious pilot take you on exciting trips to see the positive tree of life. Keep every detail of this magnificent tree forever in your mind's eye. Particularly remember, there is a special branch reserved for every Earthling. However, you need the powerful current of positive thinking to connect you with the eternal, life-giving elements of the trunk. There you will find the storehouse of treasures to cure the sick world. Your perpetual positive thinking will lead you to these hidden discoveries. Each and every one of you possesses a remarkable device within that can definitely create a positive world of good for yourself and your beloved Mother Earth.

Yet we see most negative Earthlings throw up their arms in a gesture of total despair over the present world conditions. Every dark newspaper headline and TV and radio news broadcast makes them feel even more desperate and unable to cope with the mounting problems. Many of these good people sincerely believe that the only concrete solution is to have Christ come back to personally straighten out the mess. Let us pause for a moment to take a close look at the above proposal from God's point of view. If you were in Christ's shoes, would you really be so eager to return to the planet of your cruel crucifixion? Do not forget for even a moment that you, I, and every past, present, and future Earthling equally shares in the guilt of this terrible atrocity. You see, God's divine mind could see in a flash all of our evil, negative acts from the beginning till the end of time. He also knew that only a very small minority of His people would express personal gratitude for their redemption, immortality, and for His Spirit living within them. Likewise, only another minute percentage would show their special appreciation for Christ's love, friendship, and positive teachings. I am quite sure Jesus must be very aware, too, that most of us fail to treasure and revere the priceless gifts of free will and our great computer minds. Because of the above assumptions, I personally doubt that our Lord and Savior will be in a big hurry to bail us out of our negative difficulties. God probably feels we already have the excellent equipment to do the job ourselves. What is your opinion? Promise me you will give this matter serious thought.

I honestly believe that there are only two conditions which will decide Christ's Second Coming. First, He will come to comfort and reward His small band of faithful followers, who will have suffered the horrendous, negative end of the world. At this particular time, He will also expose the negative Earthlings, whose continuous bad thinking eventually caused the total destruction of the planet Earth. Likewise, He will pass His final judgement on the entire human race. Second, He will come to rejoice in the jubilant celebration of the Earth's return to the positive. I feel with every atom of my being that the second reason will most definitely warrant His next personal appearance. So let us start this very moment to prepare for this great event. We must unite together for the chief purpose of setting the world on fire with the spirit of positive thinking. Oh, if you only knew the beauty and wonder awaiting you in the new, positive world of the future! I am sure not one of you would hesitate another minute to change your way of thinking.

However, it is understandable that some of you may have doubts about the success of this simple method. If you happen to be one of these people, I highly recommend you give the positive way of life a fair trial—even if you are doing it solely to prove the theory wrong. There is absolutely no

color; their skin will remain moist and smooth. Their posture will be erect and their muscles will stay strong and healthy for the duration of life. Remember, each and every one of you can consciously control the youthful, healthy laboratory of your subconscious mind. This great spiritual and mental part of you has the power to create all the nutrients and chemicals needed to keep your mind and body eternally young. Therefore, you can look forward to the new, positive people of Earth becoming the ageless wonders of the world. The proven evidence of the above scientific facts will be another definite, outward sign of the earth's return to the positive.

Very soon, our talented scientists will find the important key that will unlock the secret door of communication with all living matter. We will learn to master the special language of every species of nature. In other words, we shall be able to talk intelligently to all animals, birds, fish, insects and plants in their own native tongue. Likewise, they will be able to speak fluently to us. At last we shall be able to reach out with our love and friendship to every member of Mother Earth's family. This will serve to broaden our understanding and alert us immediately to everyone's needs. Everything living will soon find its rightful place of dignity and distinction in the new, positive society. For example, we shall even discover an element of good in snakes, rodents, flies, mosquitos and cockroaches. All living matter will gradually return to its original status of serving the Divine Creator's primary purpose for its existence. Little by little, you will see your beloved Mother Earth reverting to the beautiful, carefree days of the Garden of Paradise. This reverse rotation of the earth's axis will turn out to be the most positive direction our planet will have ever taken. Thus, we will definitely know the earth is getting closer to the positive when wild animals, birds, fishes, and insects stop running fearfully away from us.

Above all, our ultimate victory over the communication

barrier will lead us to a multitude of even greater achievements. Through the united power of our great computer minds we shall be able to forever erase the ugly stigma of starvation, poverty and pollution from the face of Mother Earth. We shall come up with seemingly simple solutions to all the major problems that have plagued the world ever since Adam and Eve gave birth to negative thinking. The unanimous pledge to wipe out the evil of negativism will, indeed, shower a very special blessing upon the earth. Our crops will no longer be forced to curl up and die due to lack of rain and imperfect temperatures. Through the giant media of total, conscious, positive thoughts, we will be able to subconsciously create ideal weather conditions in every country of the world. The day this prediction comes to pass will be another living symbol of the earth's eventual return to being a positive planet.

The new, positive-minded people of Earth will forever bury their depressing memories of perpetual negative thinking. This will enable them to start out with a fresh approach, bristling with the life-giving elements of positivism. They will actually achieve a rebirth in the beautiful spirit of good thoughts. The soothing balm of unanimous positive thinking will caress Mother Earth and will forever remove the obstacles of negativism. Just imagine the tremendous power of harmonious minds working together for the common good of the entire world. Earthlings can eagerly look forward to their entrance into a new, exciting, enlightened age of spectacular achievements.

Perpetual positive thinking will definitely increase our intelligence and productivity. Our brains will be able to absorb more material in less time. Therefore, it will be possible to accomplish more in shorter periods. Thus, in tomorrow's positive world, the hours spent in school and at work will be drastically cut. Everyone will enjoy greater freedom to do his own thing. Yet we will eventually become the brightest and most outstanding people of all time, thanks to the correct use of our great computer minds.

Through our unity of total positive thinking, we will succeed in tapping the treasures of the Divine Spirit within us. This will turn on the entirety of Earth's creative, inventive genius. For example, a very simple solution will be found to alleviate the energy crisis. We will learn how to convert many of our present natural resources into low-cost fuel. Scientists will also discover the means to harness the energy from the sun. In an unbelievably short period of time, Earthlings will perfect their first successful flying saucer. This will open the door to the exciting prospects of long term outer space flights. Very soon, we shall be setting foot on the unknown planet hidden behind the sun which I believe is Mother Earth's twin sister. The beautiful, friendly, God-loving inhabitants of this positive planet will give us the abundant harvest of their superior knowledge. They will point out the greatest treasure we have on Earth. It is the vibrant spirit of God living in the heart of every Earthling. We shall also be shown how to naturally control the earth's population explosion through subconscious perception. This positive solution and a multitude of other blessings will be brought back to Mother Earth. They will greatly benefit and enrich her. The actual occurrence of the above events will give living testimony to the earth's return to the positive.

Understand, I am just as eager as you are to live in the new, wonderful world of tomorrow created by our unanimous positive thinking. However, we shall never achieve a totally positive planet until we accept Almighty God, Creator of the universe, in His complete totality, minus any negative reservations whatsoever. While positive thoughts are, indeed, the stepping stones to God, any doubt about Him causes us to gradually slip back to our old, negative way of life. I am sure deception is one of Satan's favorite weapons. He has been successfully using it ever since he fathered the first negative thought. The only way you can become invincible to his future attacks is to empty every ounce of your negative concepts about God completely out of your mind. You must vouch to forever remain the living, positive chalice of His Divine truths. Remember, this is not only the responsibility of rabbis, ministers, priests, sisters, brothers, all spiritual leaders and teachers. Every Earthling is looked upon as the temple of the living God. Therefore, it is the sacred duty of each individual to revere and respect the Spirit of God within him. We must make God come alive in the world through our positive, good thoughts, words, and actions. However, the continuous good example of our beloved clergymen is, indeed, vitally necessary in achieving Earth's positive victory. They must become carbon copies of the Earthling, Jesus Christ, the living God, in their thoughts, words and actions. This will certainly extinguish the world's negative cry that God is dead.

You must realize that it is utterly impossible to understand the mysterious life of God on a human level. There is no person on Earth who has complete access to the supernatural knowledge of Divinity. Only God can really explain it to you. Therefore, the only positive alternative is to believe it without negative questioning. The following mysteries are sometimes very difficult for us to understand: (1) the Divine Creator's miraculous power to make the entire universe from the very beginning out of complete nothingness; (2) the trinity of three separate, distinct persons, Father, Son, and Holy Spirit, all being the one and same God; (3) the incarnation of Almighty God in the person of the Earthling, Christ (actually the Son of the first person of the Blessed Trinity but just as much God as His Father); (4) God the Holy Spirit, who has the unique, divine ability to be in Heaven and on Earth at the same time. He was with Jesus every moment He lived here on Earth. Ten days after Christ's ascension into Heaven, the Holy Spirit was sent back to the planet Earth to remain with the established church until the end of time (yet this third person of the Blessed Trinity is as equally God as the Father and the Son; also living in the mind of every

Earthling). Remember, the totality of God and the total spirit of positivism is one and the same. It is utterly impossible to separate them.

Please let me open up your minds and hearts to the real meaning of Christ's crucifixion. Look upon it as an important part of the divine plan to bring salvation to the world. Just remember, no Earthling could have ever prevented its occurrence. Therefore, no specific race of people, special religious group or particular country should be held responsible for it. Every Earthling must equally share in the guilt of Jesus Christ's horrible death. The only exception is Mary, the mother of Jesus. This God-man Christ not only died for the people of that time, but for all who lived before and after. His destiny was to become our Savior and Redeemer, and nothing we could have done on a human level could have changed his divine mission. Every Earthling must have Christ's key of redeeming merits from His cross in order to open the door of eternal life. Thus, we must banish every negative misconception about divine truths to become God's positive people of Earth. Your personal reluctance to do so may cause the permanent loss of tomorrow's new world. How many of you really want to take such a serious risk? Would it not be a much better idea for you to become like a little child again in spirit, thereby accepting God in His positive good of complete totality?

Just look at the loving care we give the helpless newborn infant. We certainly would not expect him to immediately take care of himself independently. Maturity is a slow, gradual process, as is our spiritual development. For this good reason, God wants us to start growing with Him at the very beginning. This means carefully following His path of personal revelation step by step through the entire Old Testament. Little by little, His true identity will be made known to us. It will not be too difficult during this early period of spiritual growth to accept Him as God, our loving Father. Gradually, we are prepared to go beyond the Father's image to find the one and the same God in the promised Messiah, Jesus Christ. Much later Christ enables us to clearly see this one and the same God of the Father and the Son in the Holy Spirit. Remember, without the primary knowledge of God in the Old Testament, we can never reach our complete fulfillment of Him in the New Testament.

God has really closer contact with us today than during the time He spent here on Earth in the human form of an Earthling. His Holy Spirit has been very active in the world ever since the day Jesus sent Him to remain with us forever. Likewise, Christ's living presence is found in the consecrated bread and wine on the altars of His established church in most of the countries of the world. It is possible for Jesus to live within each and every one of you. He wants so very much to make the temple of your body His permanent, happy home. However, you must depend upon your perpetual good thoughts to open up the gates of your mind and heart wide enough to let Jesus in. Just think how fortunate you will be to have Christ as your honored guest. How you will treasure His living spirit! He will change you into a new, wonderful person. Everyone will see Him in you and you will also be aware of the reflection of His image in every person you meet. Now let us go a step beyond the ordinary, into the divine realm of supreme ecstasy, by surrendering yourself completely to Jesus. This means your sincere pledge of total commitment to Him for the rest of your life. From this glorious moment, all of your thoughts, words, and actions will automatically be His. If we could only get enough people to give this positive, spontaneous response to Him. It would indeed be possible for the earth to become the planet of the living Christ.

God wishes us to give continuous reverence to His indwelling spirit and, likewise, to His living presence in the entire world. Above all, every Earthling must accept Jesus Christ, the living God, as his Savior and Redeemer. It is also necessary to fervently believe all divine revealed truths without negative exception. The moment each and every one of you adheres to the above beliefs, the earth will definitely return to her original positive status. From this day forward, I know all of you will do everything within your power to help the earth to become a positive planet again. I fully expect Jesus to fly back to Earth to celebrate this jubilant occasion with us. However, there will be certain positive, outward signs which will not only prepare the world for this great day, but also for Christ's Second Coming. I am going to describe them in intricate detail. So please read the following very carefully.

The eve before this dual celebration and, likewise, during the entire day, a spectacular phenomenon will appear in the sky. It will be visible from every corner of the earth. A beautiful woman will be seen dressed in white, holding a Rosary made out of stars in her right hand, in her left hand will be held a huge brown scapular, and around her neck will be a gleaming chain as bright as the sun. The attached illuminated miraculous medal covering her pure heart will emit sparkling rays of God's special blessings to Earth. A man with dark hair, moustache, short beard and roughened hands will be standing beside her. The sun, moon, and stars will revolve around them and actually touch the ground. This will symbolize the earth's complete purification for God's arrival. However, one large star in the east will remain stationary. This is the same star that led the wisemen to the Christ Child. Now we shall follow it again to reach Christ's landing place, which will be the first country in the world that unanimously achieved all of His positive requirements. Suddenly a bright spotlight will miraculously project from the same eastern star and will shine brilliantly on the handsome couple in the center. Everyone will immediately recognize them to be Mary, the mother of Jesus, and Joseph the carpenter, His foster father. It is only fitting that they should witness their divine Son's glorious return to earth.

Looking toward the east, we shall see a large, fleecy, white cloud approaching the earth. Very soon, to our great surprise, we shall find more occupants on it than we were originally expecting. Our very first glimpse will be of a kindly older man with white hair, full moustache, and long beard. I believe this is God the Father, the first person of the blessed trinity. Sitting next to Him will be a virile, youthful, handsome man, who is most assuredly Jesus Christ, the living God, second person of the Blessed Trinity. Above the Father and the Son's heads is a beautiful white dove, representing God the Holy Spirit, the third person of the Blessed Trinity. Just imagine, God in His complete totality of the Trinity will personally come to reward His positive-minded people of Earth.

At this breathtaking moment, we shall hear the beautiful choir of angels singing, "Rejoice, rejoice on this glorious day of the Earth's return to the positive. Your total God is coming down from Heaven for a twofold purpose. He wants to celebrate this great day by revealing Himself to you in His entirety." Every Earthling will sing out, "Yes, we are rejoicing over the visitation of the Blessed Trinity and our supreme victory of returning the Earth to the positive. Look! We're welcoming God, the Light of the World, with our perpetual positive shine."

Then the Trinity will land on the pure ground of the first country of the world that successfully achieved total positive thinking. God will express His deep appreciation by bestowing a very special blessing upon these good people. However, everyone in the world will see Him and hear His voice.

Michael, Gabriel, and Raphael will personally escort Mary and Joseph down from the sky. They will be given places of honor in the receiving line, standing next to their divine Son. The Blessed Trinity, Mary, Joseph, and the archangels will joyfully greet all the positive people of Earth. Jesus will speak words of love and praise to His fellow Earthlings. He will especially thank them for their good, positive thoughts, which have led them to accept all of His divine truths and positive teachings. Above all, He will acknowledge His deep gratitude for their heroic work of returning the earth to its original positive status. Then He will announce the good news, that our bodies will no longer have to die. Our unanimous positive thoughts have finally succeeded in creating Heaven on Earth. At the triumphant sound of the trumpets, God the Father will tell the angels to open up the gates of Heaven. The beautiful white dove, signifying the Holy Spirit, will fly to meet the multitudes of heavenly Earthlings. He will lead the return flight of our loved ones back to Earth. From this great moment of unity and forever and ever, Heaven and Earth will be one and the same place.

You see, each and every one of you has the positive power to make your beloved Mother Earth exactly like Heaven. Remember, just by the simple act of thinking good, positive thoughts, you not only change yourself, but also the world. I know I can count on all of you to do your part to eventually make the earth a totally positive planet. It is definitely possible to create this magnificent new world of tomorrow with your positive, good thoughts today. Nothing is impossible with God. Therefore, nothing should be impossible for you, because He lives within your mind.

So we can easily sum up this entire book in just a few short sentences. Always think good, positive thoughts. They will automatically influence your words, responses, and actions. Above all, they will lead you to accept the totality of God and His positive teachings without any negative reservations.

I want you to know that all the personal beliefs contained in this book come to you straight from my heart. How happy it makes me to know I have helped you to turn on your personal channel of positive thinking. I shall never have to say good-bye, because my good thoughts will always be with you. I am sure I can count on yours being with me, too.